W9-BHS-756

Egypt

Sue Townsend and Caroline Young

Heinemann Library
Chicago, Illinois

Customer Service 888-454-2279

Visit our website at
www.heinemannlibrary.com

Designed by Jo Hinton-Malivoire and
Tinstar Design Limited (www.tinstar.co.uk)
Illustrations by Nicholas Beresford-Davies
Originated by Dot Gradations Ltd
Printed in China
by Wing King Tong

07 06 05 04 03
10 9 8 7 6 5 4 3 2 1

**Library of Congress Cataloging-in-
Publication Data**
Townsend, Sue, 1963-
  Egypt / Sue Townsend and Caroline Young.
    p. cm. -- (A world of recipes)
Summary: Presents recipes from Egypt that
reflect the ingredients and culture of the
country.
Includes bibliographical references and index.
  ISBN 1-4034-0979-X
  1. Cookery, Egyptian--Juvenile literature. [1.
Cookery, Egyptian. 2.
Food habits--Egypt.] I. Young, Caroline, 1939-
II. Title.
  TX725.E35T69 2003
  641.5962--dc21

2002155855

Acknowledgments
The author and publishers are grateful to the
following for permission to reproduce
copyright material: p. 5 Corbis; all other
photographs Gareth Boden.

Cover photographs reproduced with
permission of Gareth Boden.

The publishers would like to thank Wafa
Iskander for her assistance with the
preparation of this book.

Every effort has been made to contact
copyright holders of any material reproduced
in this book. Any omissions will be rectified in
subsequent printings if notice is given to the
publisher.

Some words are shown in
bold, **like this.** You can find
out what they mean by
looking in the glossary.

Contents

Key

* easy

** medium

*** difficult

Egyptian Food

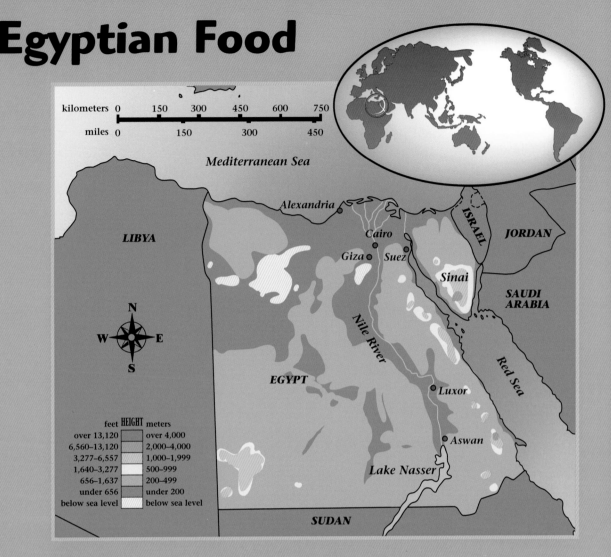

kilometers 0 150 300 450 600 750

miles 0 150 300 450

Mediterranean Sea

Alexandria

LIBYA

Cairo

Giza Suez

ISRAEL

JORDAN

Sinai

SAUDI ARABIA

Nile River

N
W E
S

EGYPT

Luxor

Red Sea

feet HEIGHT meters	
over 13,120	over 4,000
6,560–13,120	2,000–4,000
3,277–6,557	1,000–1,999
1,640–3,277	500–999
656–1,637	200–499
under 656	under 200
below sea level	below sea level

Aswan

Lake Nasser

SUDAN

Egyptian food

Egypt is in the northeast corner of Africa. It is part of the world called the Middle East. Egypt is very dry, and about 96 percent of the land is desert. The peoples of the Middle East share many customs and cooking styles, but each has their own rich traditions.

In the past

About 5,000 years ago, the ancient Egyptians built a great civilization. Massive stone pyramids were built as tombs for the Egyptian kings, called pharaohs (*fair-ohs*). Some still stand today. After about 3,000 years, the pharaohs' power faded, and in the 1st century B.C.E., Egypt became part of the Roman Empire. After the collapse of Roman rule, the following centuries saw Arab princes, Turkish Ottoman emperors, the French leader Napoleon Bonaparte, and the British all ruling Egypt at different times. Today, Egypt is called the Arab Republic of Egypt, and most of its people follow the Muslim religion.

Fruits and vegetables are sold in this weekly Egyptian market.

Around the country

Deserts cover most of Egypt, except for a small, **fertile** strip of land along the Nile River. The Nile Delta (the triangular area of land where the Nile flows into the Mediterranean Sea) is especially important for its farmland. Most Egyptians live by farming the land near the river and catching fish in its waters. When the Nile River overflows its banks in late summer, it floods the land around it. The floodwater leaves behind a layer of rich soil that is good for planting crops. Egyptian farmers grow many kinds of fruits, including dates, grapes, and apricots. They also grow grains, such as barley, wheat, and rice, and many kinds of vegetables, too.

Egyptian meals

Because it is so hot in the middle of the day, people in Egypt usually eat their main meal in mid-afternoon. Breakfast might be yogurt, bread, and fruit. Lunch might be a selection of small dishes called *mezzeh* (pronounced *mezz-uh*), served with plenty of bread. In villages, several dishes are put in bowls in the center of a low table. People sit on cushions, helping themselves to some of each dish. Supper is usually a light meal of yogurt, semit (soft pretzels covered with sesame seeds), eggs, and fruit.

Ingredients

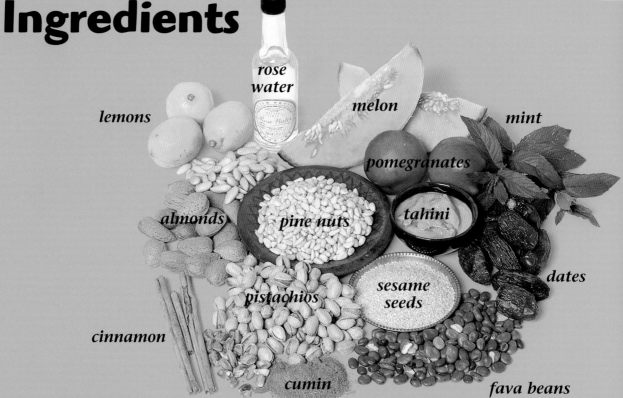

rose water

lemons

melon

mint

pomegranates

almonds

pine nuts

tahini

pistachios

sesame seeds

dates

cinnamon

cumin

fava beans

Beans

Many Egyptian recipes contain beans, including brown fava beans. Most dried beans must be soaked in cold water overnight, **boiled** for 10 minutes, and then **simmered** until soft before you can use them. Using canned beans saves time. Large grocery stores and health–food shops sell dried and canned beans.

Cinnamon

Cinnamon comes from the bark of a tree. It has a warm, spicy flavor and is often added to sweet dishes, such as pastries. You can buy it in sticks (which are the curled-up tree bark), or **ground**.

Cumin

Cumin is a spice used to flavor many dishes. We know that Egyptian cooks used cumin more than 3,000 years ago, because **archaeologists** found some at the pyramids. Buy it as seeds, or ground, from grocery stores.

Dates

The sweet, brown fruits of the date palm tree are called dates. They have a pit in them. Many grocery stores sell fresh dates in winter, and dried dates year-round.

Nuts

Some Egyptian recipes use almonds, which you can buy blanched (without their skins), **flaked**, ground, or **chopped.** Others use green pistachio nuts, or pine nuts. Grocery stores sell them all.

Pomegranates

The pomegranate fruit is in season from October to December. Pomegranates have a tough skin and lots of bittersweet, fleshy seeds inside. Large grocery stores sell them when they are in season.

Rose water

Rose water is a delicately scented liquid made from the petals of roses. Look for it in health–food stores or pharmacies. If you cannot find it, use almond essence or orange–flower water instead.

Sesame seeds

Sesame seeds add a nutty flavor to dishes, especially when **toasted**. The seeds are also made into sesame oil, which adds a strong, rich flavor when used for **frying**. Buy sesame seeds and sesame oil from grocery stores.

Tahini

Tahini is a stiff paste made by mixing ground, toasted sesame seeds with sesame oil or olive oil. Stir it before you use it. Health–food stores or grocery stores sell tahini.

Before You Start

Kitchen rules

There are a few basic rules you should always follow when you are cooking:

- Ask an adult if you can use the kitchen.
- Some cooking processes, especially those involving hot water or oil, can be dangerous. When you see this sign, take extra care or ask an adult to help.
- Wash your hands before you start.
- Wear an apron to protect your clothes.
- Be very careful when you use sharp knives.
- Never leave pan handles sticking out because you might bump into them and spill hot food.
- Use oven mitts to lift things in and out of the oven.
- Wash fruits and vegetables before you use them.
- Always wash chopping boards very well after use, especially after chopping raw meat, fish, or poultry.
- Use a separate chopping board for onions and garlic, if possible.

How long will it take?

Some of the recipes in this book are quick and easy, and some are more difficult and take longer. The stripe across the right-hand side of each recipe page tells you how long it takes to prepare a dish from start to finish. It also shows how difficult each recipe is to make: * (easy), ** (medium), or *** (difficult).

Quantities and measurements

You can see how many people each recipe will serve at the top of each right-hand page. You can multiply or divide the quantities if you want to cook for more or fewer people.

Ingredients for recipes can be measured in two ways. Imperial measurements use cups and ounces. Metric measurements use grams and milliliters.

In the recipes, you will see the following abbreviations:

tbsp = tablespoon   oz = ounce   cm = centimeter
tsp = teaspoon   lb = pound   g = gram
ml = milliliter   in. = inch

Utensils

To cook the recipes in this book, you will need these utensils (as well as essentials, such as spoons, plates, and bowls):

- plastic or glass chopping board (much easier to clean than a wooden one)
- food processor or blender
- large frying pan
- 9-in. (23-cm) non-stick frying pan with a lid
- measuring cup
- spatula
- 2½ cup (600 ml) ovenproof dish
- sieve
- small and large saucepans

- set of scales
- sharp knife
- baking sheets
- garlic crusher
- melon baller
- 10-in (25-cm) loose-bottomed cake tin
- metal **skewers**
- baking parchment
- slotted spoon

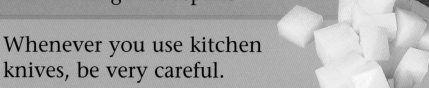

! Whenever you use kitchen knives, be very careful.

Broad Bean Rissoles

This recipe is made slightly differently in each Middle Eastern country. The Egyptian version is called *Ta'Amiah* (pronounced *ta-mih-ya*), and is made with dried, white broad beans. Use two 15-oz (440-g) cans of the beans and start the recipe at step 3, if you prefer. Serve the rissoles as a snack with salad.

What you need

15 oz (440 g) dried
  white broad beans
2 cloves garlic
1 onion
½ of a lemon
1 tsp **ground** cumin
1 tsp ground cilantro
½ tsp dried oregano
1 tbsp fresh cilantro
1 tbsp tahini
1 tbsp flour
3 tbsp olive oil or
  vegetable oil

To garnish:
Fresh cilantro leaves

What you do

1 Put the beans into a colander. Rinse them under running cold water.

2 Put them into a bowl and cover with plenty of cold water. Leave the beans to soak overnight.

3 **Drain** and rinse the beans well. **Blend** them in a food processor or blender until coarsely ground.

4 **Peel** and finely **chop** the garlic and onion.

5 Using a lemon squeezer, squeeze the juice from the half-lemon.

6 Add the garlic, onion, lemon juice, ground spices, oregano, fresh cilantro, and tahini to the blender.

7 Blend until the mixture is quite firm and not crumbly (add a little water if necessary).

8 Sprinkle a work surface and your hands with the flour. In your hands, shape 1½ tbsp of the mixture into a ball, and then flatten it with your palm into a teardrop-shaped rissole.

9 Repeat this process with the rest of the mixture.

⊘ **10** Heat half of the oil in a large frying pan over medium heat. **Fry** half the number of rissoles for 3 minutes on each side, until browned.

11 Using a spatula, lift them onto paper towel to drain. Heat the remaining oil and cook the rest of the rissoles.

12 Serve the rissoles hot, garnished with fresh cilantro.

Eggplant Dip

Egyptian meals often begin with a selection of small dishes. They are served to sharpen the diners' appetites for the main course. This eggplant dip is delicious served with warmed pita bread.

What you need

2 eggplants
2 tsp **ground** cumin
1 clove garlic
1 tbsp lemon juice
4 tbsp tahini
8 pita breads
1 tbsp chopped
   fresh parsley

*To **garnish**:*
Wedge of lemon

What you do

1 **Preheat** the oven to 400°F (200°C).
Put the eggplants on a baking tray, and **bake** for 30 minutes.

2 **Dry-fry** the cumin in a small frying pan over medium heat for 30 seconds. Pour it into a bowl.

3 **Peel** and finely **chop** the garlic. Add it to the cumin with the lemon juice and tahini.

4 When the eggplants are cool, cut them in half. Scoop the flesh into a blender or food processor.

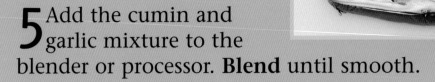

5 Add the cumin and garlic mixture to the blender or processor. **Blend** until smooth.

6 Spoon the mixture into a bowl. **Cover** with plastic wrap, and **chill** for 1 hour.

7 **Toast** some pita bread in a toaster until they are lightly browned.

(!) **8** Using a dish towel to protect your hands from hot steam, lift the pita breads onto a chopping board. Cut them into wide strips.

9 Repeat steps 7 and 8 with the rest of the pita bread.

10 Chop the fresh parsley and stir it into the chilled dip. Put the bowl of dip onto a large plate and serve, surrounded by pita bread strips and garnished with a wedge of lemon.

STARTERS SELECTION

For a really Egyptian selection of starters, try serving Eggplant Dip with Semit (page 14), Cheese and Egg Pastries (page 16), Broad Bean Rissoles (page 10), and some fresh olives.

Semit (Sesame Rings)

Street vendors in Cairo, the capital city of Egypt, sell freshly made *semit* (pronounced *sem-iht*) as a take-out snack. They are ideal spread with butter, or served with jam or cheese.

What you need

½ oz (10 g) dried yeast
Pinch of sugar
½ cup (100 ml) milk
1 oz (25 g) butter
1 tbsp sugar
1 tsp salt
14 oz (400 g) plain flour
2 ¼-cups (50 ml each) of
    warm water
Vegetable oil for
    brushing
1 egg
6 tbsp sesame seeds

What you do

1 Put ¼ cup (50 ml) warm water into a cup. The water should feel the same temperature as your finger.

2 Stir in the yeast and a pinch of sugar until they **dissolve**. Leave the cup somewhere warm for 20 minutes.

(!) 3 Warm the milk in a saucepan. Add ¼ cup (50 ml) water, butter, sugar, and salt, and stir. Pour this mixture into a large bowl. When it feels "finger-warm," stir in the yeast mixture.

4 Stir the flour into the liquid with a wooden spoon. Using your hands, make the dough into a soft, but not sticky, ball.

5 Sprinkle a little flour onto a work surface. Stretch the dough out, then fold it in half. Turn it, then stretch it again and fold. **Knead** like this for 5 minutes.

6 Put the dough into a bowl. **Cover** with a dish towel, and leave somewhere warm for 30 minutes.

7 Brush a little oil onto two baking sheets.

8 Knead the dough again for 10 minutes. Divide it into eight pieces.

9 Shape one piece into a sausage shape about 8-in. (20-cm) long. Dip one end in water, pinch the two ends together and shape into a ring. Make seven more rings.

10 **Beat** the egg with 1 tbsp water. Brush it over the dough rings, and sprinkle with sesame seeds.

11 Lay the rings 2 in. (5 cm) apart on baking sheets. Cover with the dish towel, and leave in a warm place for 40 minutes, until doubled in size. **Preheat** the oven to 450°F (220°C).

12 **Bake** the dough rings for 12–15 minutes, until they are golden. Lift them onto a wire rack to cool. Serve after cooling.

Cheese and Egg Pastries

In Egypt, people often make their own soft cheese. It tastes a little like the Greek cheese, feta. Use feta cheese to make these pastries, called *sambusak* (pronounced *sam-buh-sak*) in Egypt.

What you need

For the filling:
1 egg
4 oz (100 g) feta cheese

For the pastry:
3 oz (75 g) butter
6 tbsp olive oil
½ tsp salt
8 oz (225 g) plain flour
2 tbsp plain flour (for sprinkling on baking sheets and work surface)
6 tbsp water
1 egg
2 tbsp sesame seeds

What you do

1 Make the filling first. Put the egg into a small pan of water. Bring to a **boil**, and boil for 8 minutes.

2 Using a slotted spoon, lift the egg into a pan of cold water, and leave it to cool.

3 Peel off the shell. Put the egg and feta cheese into a small bowl. Use a knife to **chop** them finely against the side of the bowl, until you have a crumbly mixture.

4 To make the pastry, melt the butter in a small pan over low heat. Pour it into another bowl, and add the oil, 6 tbsp water, and salt.

5 Stir the flour into the oil mixture until it forms a ball of dough.

6 **Preheat** the oven to 375°F (190°C). Sprinkle 1 tbsp flour over two baking sheets.

7 With your hands, shape 2 tbsp of the dough into a ball. Sprinkle a little flour onto a work surface, and roll the ball with a rolling pin until it is a 3-in. (8-cm) circle. Lift each onto a baking sheet.

8 Put 1 tsp of the egg mixture into the center of the circle. Brush a little water around the edge. Fold one side across to the other, and pinch the edges together to make your first pastry.

9 Repeat steps 7 to 9 to make more pastries.

10 **Beat** the second egg, and brush it over each pastry. Sprinkle with sesame seeds.

(!) 11 **Bake** the pastries for 20 minutes, until golden.

12 Cool on a wire rack, and serve hot or cold.

Egyptian Bread

On an average day, enough bread is sold in Egypt for each person to have three small loaves. This recipe is for bread called *aiysh* (pronounced *ayesh*) in Egypt. It puffs up when cooked, and is often used for scooping up food.

What you need

¼-oz (7-g) sachet easy blend dried yeast
13 oz (350 g) whole wheat flour
4 oz (100 g) plain flour
2 cups (460 ml) warm water

What you do

1 Put the yeast and both kinds of flour into a bowl. Stir them well.

2 Pour 2 cups (460 ml) warm water into a cup. If you dip your finger into it, it should feel the same temperature as your finger.

3 Stir the water into the yeast and flour mixture. Use your hands to make a soft, but not sticky, ball of dough.

4 Sprinkle some flour onto a work surface. Stretch the dough out, then fold it in half. Turn it, then stretch and fold again. **Knead** like this for 10 minutes, until the dough is smooth.

5 Put the dough back into the bowl. **Cover** with a clean dish towel, and leave somewhere warm for 1 hour, until it has doubled in size.

6 Knead the dough on a floured surface for 5 minutes. Cut the dough into twelve pieces.

7 Using a rolling pin, roll each piece into a thin 8-in. (20-cm) circle.

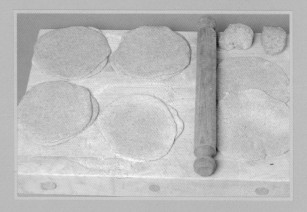

8 Put one circle on top of another, and press the edges together with your fingers. Repeat to make six circles.

9 Put the circles on to baking trays, leaving 2 in. (5 cm) between them.

10 Cover them with a clean dish towel, and leave in a warm place to rise for 40 minutes. **Preheat** the oven to 400°F (200°C).

11 Put the baking trays into the oven, and **bake** the bread for 8 minutes, until puffed up and golden.

12 Leave the loaves on the baking trays to cool. Serve the same day.

Onion Omelette

People in Egypt eat a lot of eggs. A favorite way of serving them is in an omelette, called an *eggah* in Egypt. They are ideal as a snack or light lunch, with some bread and a salad.

What you need

Half an onion
2 eggs
4 tbsp fresh parsley
1 tbsp butter

*To **garnish:***
Sprigs of parsley

What you do

1 **Peel** the half-onion and **chop** it.

2 Crack the eggs into a bowl. **Beat** them lightly with a fork.

3 Chop the parsley on a chopping board.

4 Melt the butter in an 8-in. (20-cm) frying pan over medium heat.

(!) 5 **Fry** the onion over medium to low heat for about 3 minutes, or until it has softened.

6 Using a slotted spoon, lift half the fried onion into a bowl.

7 Pour the beaten egg into the pan. Tilt the pan so that egg covers the whole of the base of the pan.

8 Cook for 3 minutes until the surface of the egg starts to set.

9 Sprinkle the rest of the cooked onion over the omelette. Fold it in half, using a spatula.

10 Carefully slide the omelette onto a warmed plate, and serve garnished with fresh parsley.

DIFFERENT FILLINGS

You could add **flaked**, cooked fish, or chopped, cooked chicken, to your omelette, if you wish.

Fattosh (Crunchy Salad)

It is so hot during the day in Egypt that people usually only eat a light lunch, such as a salad. This popular salad recipe is called *fattosh* (pronounced *fat-tush*). It uses three fresh herbs, each one adding a slightly different flavor.

What you need

1 cucumber
6 tomatoes
1 bunch green onions
1 yellow pepper
1 tbsp fresh parsley
1 tbsp fresh cilantro
1 tbsp fresh mint
2 or 3 slices of bread
 or pita breads

*For the **dressing**:*
1 clove garlic
4 tbsp olive oil
1 lemon

What you do

1 Trim both ends off the cucumber. Cut it in half lengthwise, then into quarters. Cut each quarter into chunks.

2 Cut the tomatoes into quarters, and then into chunks.

3 Trim off the roots and dark green tops of the green onions. Cut the green onions into thin **slices**.

4 Cut the pepper in half, throwing away the stalk and the seeds. Cut the flesh into chunks.

5 **Chop** the fresh parsley, cilantro, and mint finely. Put them and the vegetables you have cut up into a bowl.

6 **Cover** the bowl with plastic wrap, and put it in the refrigerator.

7 Meanwhile, **peel** and crush the garlic in a garlic crusher. Put the garlic into a small, screw-topped jar with the olive oil.

8 Using a lemon squeezer, squeeze the juice from the lemon. Add it and some salt and pepper to the jar, and screw the lid on tightly.

(!) 9 **Toast** the bread or pita bread until lightly browned. Tear it into pieces, and **toss** it into the salad.

10 Shake the dressing in the jar. Pour the dressing over the salad and serve.

Goat's Cheese and Mint Salad

Many Egyptian farmers keep goats for their milk and their meat. People drink the milk, or make it into soft, white cheese. Goat's cheese has a strong, tangy flavor that goes well with the fresh salad.

What you need

10 oz (300 g) firm goat's cheese
2 tbsp plain flour
1 egg
2 oz (50 g) fresh bread crumbs
1 tsp fresh thyme
4 tbsp olive oil
4 tomatoes
1 onion
1 clove garlic
1 tbsp olive oil
6 tbsp fresh mint

What you do

1 Cut the goat's cheese into eight thick **slices**. **Dust** each slice with flour on both sides.

2 **Beat** the egg, and pour it into a shallow bowl.

3 Mix the bread crumbs and thyme together, and put them on a plate.

4 Dip each slice of cheese into the egg, and then into the bread crumbs, **coating** them well.

5 Place the coated cheese slices on a plate, and **chill**.

6 Meanwhile, make the salad. **Chop** the tomatoes. **Peel** and finely chop the onion and garlic. Put the tomatoes, onion, garlic, and olive oil into a bowl.

7 Tear the mint leaves and add them to the bowl. **Toss** the salad well and put it onto four plates.

(!) 8 Put 4 tbsp oil in a frying pan and heat over medium heat for 1 minute. **Fry** the chilled goat's cheese slices for 2 minutes on each side, until they are golden.

9 Using a spatula, put two to three slices of cheese on top of each plate of salad. Serve immediately.

AMAZING GOATS

Goats prefer a hot, dry climate, such as that in Egypt. They eat weeds, shrubs, and other plants, rather than just grass. Goat's milk is easily digested, and has more **protein** and fat than that of cows.

Fava Bean Stew

Egyptians cook beans in a tall, thin pot called an *idra* (pronounced *id-rah*). It has a tight-fitting lid that keeps the steam and moisture in the pot. This stops the beans from drying up as they cook.

What you need

10 oz (300 g) dried fava beans or other dried beans
4 cloves garlic
2 onions
2 tbsp olive oil
1 tsp **ground** cumin
Small pinch ground cinnamon
Small pinch of ground allspice
A pinch of salt
2 tbsp fresh parsley

To garnish:
Lemon wedges

What you do

1 Rinse the beans in cold water. Put them in a bowl, cover with plenty of cold water, and leave in a cool place overnight.

2 **Drain** the beans. Put them into a saucepan and just cover them with water.

(!) 3 Bring to a **boil** and boil for 10 minutes. Now **cover** and **simmer** for 1½ hours, or until the beans are tender. (Add extra boiling water if the beans start to boil dry.)

4 **Peel** and finely **chop** the garlic and onions. Chop the parsley.

(!) 5 Heat the oil in a frying pan. **Fry** the garlic and onions over medium heat until they are golden brown.

6 Stir in the ground spices. Cook for 30 seconds and take the pan off the heat.

7 Put a colander over a bowl. Drain the beans and pour them back into the pan. Keep the liquid they were cooked in.

8 Stir the spicy onion mixture, salt, parsley, and ½ cup (120 ml) of the beans' cooking liquid into the pan. Heat the mixture thoroughly.

9 Cut a lemon into wedges.

10 Spoon the beans onto a serving plate, garnish with lemon wedges, and serve with *aiysh* (page 18), pita, or another sort of bread.

Baked Fish with Nut Sauce

People in Egypt can catch freshwater fish in the Nile River, and sea fish along the country's two, long coastlines. Egyptian cooks may use carp, sea bass, bream, or gray mullet for this recipe. You can use cod, haddock, or salmon instead. Leave the skin on to keep the fish firm while it cooks.

What you need

2 oz (50 g) pine nuts
2 oz (50 g) skinned
   hazelnuts
1 onion
2 tbsp vegetable oil
1 tbsp fresh parsley
14 oz (400 g) can
   chopped tomatoes
4 fish fillets weighing
   2–4 oz (50–100 g)
   each (with skin on)
1 tbsp plain flour
1 tbsp butter

To garnish:
Fresh parsley

What you do

1 Put the nuts in a small saucepan. Cook them over medium heat until they start to brown, and then pour them onto a plate.

2 **Peel** and finely **chop** the onion.

(!) 3 Heat 1 tbsp of the oil in a frying pan over medium heat. **Fry** the onion for 3 minutes, until softened.

4 Chop the parsley. Stir the parsley, tomatoes, and nuts into the onions. **Cover** and **simmer** for 5 minutes.

5 **Dust** the fleshy side of the fish with flour.

6 Heat the rest of the oil and the butter in a large frying pan over medium heat.

7 Fry the fillets for 3 minutes on each side, until the flesh **flakes** easily.

8 Put the fish on a warmed serving plate. Spoon the tomato and nut sauce over it.

9 Garnish with parsley, and serve with potatoes or rice and some vegetables.

Chicken Kebabs

Street vendors in Egypt sell kebabs tucked into pita bread as a take-out snack. Egyptian cooks might make them with chicken or pigeon meat. These chicken kebabs would be ideal for cooking on the barbecue in the summer, or placing under a broiler.

What you need

1 lb (500 g) boneless chicken portions (breast, thigh, or leg)
1 onion
1 clove garlic
4 tbsp olive oil
1 lemon
2 tsp paprika

To garnish:
Sprigs of fresh mint
1 tomato

What you do

1 Cut the chicken into 2-in. (5-cm) chunks. Put in a bowl.

2 **Peel** and finely **chop** the onion and garlic. Add them and the olive oil to the chicken.

3 Wash the lemon thoroughly and cut it into six pieces. Squeeze each piece over the chicken so that the juice goes into the bowl.

4 Stir the lemon skins into the chicken. **Cover** and **chill** for 3 hours.

5 **Preheat** the oven to 400°F (200°C). Thread the chicken chunks onto four metal **skewers**.

6 Sprinkle paprika over the chicken pieces. Lay them on a baking tray.

7 Cook the chicken in the oven for 20 minutes.

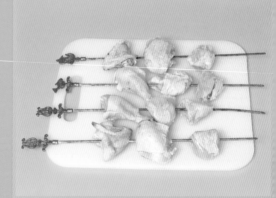

8 **Preheat** the grill or broiler to medium hot.

9 **Grill** or **broil** the chicken pieces for 5–10 minutes, until they are golden and crispy.

10 Garnish with mint and a tomato, cut into quarters. Serve the kebabs hot with rice and a salad.

EATING ON THE STREET

The streets of big Egyptian cities echo with the cries of street vendors shouting out what they are selling. Many cook the food beside the road. You can buy all sorts of traditional foods without ever going into a restaurant.

Rice with Vermicelli

Vermicelli is long, thin strands of pasta, and was first made in Italy. About 600 years ago, traders from the Italian city of Venice visited the Middle East. They introduced vermicelli to the people there. Rice with vermicelli became a traditional Egyptian dish.

What you need

7 oz (200 g) basmati or long grain rice
3 oz (75 g) vermicelli
3 tbsp olive oil
3 tbsp pine nuts

What you do

1 Put the rice into a bowl and cover it with cold water. Leave it for 30 minutes.

2 Pour the rice into a sieve and rinse it under cold water until it runs clear.

3 Break the vermicelli into ½-in. (1-cm) pieces.

4 Put a large potful of water on the stove to **boil**.

5 Heat the oil in a large saucepan over medium heat. Add the rice and vermicelli, and **stir-fry** for 2 minutes.

6 Carefully pour 3½ cups (800 ml) of boiling water from the pot into a measuring cup. Add it to the pan and stir well.

7 Bring the liquid in the pan to a boil. Now turn the heat down to low, put the lid on the pan, and **simmer** for 8 minutes.

8 Using a teaspoon, test a little of the rice to see if it is cooked. If it is not, and all the water has been soaked up, add a little extra boiling water.

9 When it is cooked, **drain** the rice, if you need to.

10 Sprinkle the rice with pine nuts and serve with another dish, such as Baked Fish with Nut Sauce (page 28) or Chicken Kebabs (page 30).

Date and Nut Pastries

Egyptian cakes and pastries tend to be extremely sweet. Many are flavored with nuts and rose water. In Egypt, people might eat a pastry with coffee after a meal, or as a quick snack.

What you need

1 oz (25 g) dried dates (with pits removed)
1 oz (25 g) blanched almonds
1 oz (25 g) shelled pistachio nuts
1 oz (25 g) soft brown sugar
½ tsp **ground** cinnamon
4 oz (100 g) unsalted butter
8 oz (225 g) plain flour
1 tbsp rose water, or a few drops of almond essence or orange-flower water
2 tbsp milk
5 tbsp water
Confectioners' sugar for **dusting**

What you do

1 **Chop** the dates and nuts into small pieces.

2 Put the dates into a pan with the sugar, cinnamon, and 5 tbsp water.

3 **Cover** and **simmer** for 5 minutes, until the water has been soaked up.

4 Stir in the chopped nuts.

5 Melt the butter in a pan over low heat.

6 **Sift** the flour into a bowl. Making cutting movements with a knife, **fold** the melted butter into the flour.

7 Stir in the rose water and milk. Squeeze the mixture into a ball.

8 **Preheat** the oven to 400°F (200°C).

9 Cut the dough into sixteen pieces.

10 Roll a piece of dough into a ball. Press your thumb into the ball, and shape the dough around it like a thimble.

11 Put some of the date and nut filling into the "thimble." Press the top edges shut.

12 Put the pastry onto a baking sheet. Use a fork to flatten it slightly, making a pattern on top.

13 Repeat steps 11 and 12 with the other pieces of dough.

14 **Bake** for 10–15 minutes, until golden brown.

15 Cool the pastries on the baking sheet for 10 minutes, and then lift them onto a wire rack. Dust with confectioners' sugar. Serve immediately, or store in an airtight container.

Um'ali (Pastry Pudding)

This Egyptian pudding is made up of layers of nuts, raisins, and spices, and cooked, crushed filo pastry. You can buy ready-made filo pastry in grocery stores. In Egypt, cooks sometimes use toasted bread, or crackers called *raqaq*, (pronounced *ru-cack*) instead.

What you need

½ cup (50 g) butter
5 oz (150 g) filo pastry
2 oz (50 g) dried dates
1 oz (25 g) pine nuts
2 oz (50 g) almonds
1 oz (25 g) pistachio nuts
1 oz (25 g) raisins
½ tsp **ground** cloves
½ tsp ground cinnamon
¼ tsp ground cardamom
7 oz (200 g) sweetened condensed milk
1 cup (240 ml) heavy cream

What you do

1 **Preheat** the oven to 400°F (200°C).

2 Melt the butter in a small pan over low heat.

3 Open the filo pastry and lay it flat. Brush the top of the filo with some melted butter, scrunch it up, and put it onto a baking sheet. (You will need two baking sheets).

4 Repeat this until all the pastry is used.

5 **Bake** the pastry in the oven for 10 minutes, until lightly browned. Leave to cool.

6 Cut each date in half and take out its pit.

7 Chop the dates and nuts, and put them in a bowl. Add the raisins and spices.

8 Crumble a third of the pastry into a 2½-cup (600-ml) ovenproof dish. Sprinkle half the nut mixture on top.

9 Scatter a third of the rest of the pastry onto the nut mixture.

10 Add the remaining nut mixture, and crumble on the rest of the pastry.

11 Put the condensed milk and cream into a pan. Warm gently over low heat until the mixture is just **simmering**—no hotter. Pour the liquid over the pastry.

12 Put the dish into the oven and bake for 20–30 minutes, until golden. Serve hot.

Date Cake

Egyptian cooks use a lot of dates, because they are so plentiful. Dates are very healthy because they are a fruit, and they are also very sweet. There are more than 300 different kinds of dates. The most expensive ones are medjool dates, which grow in Egypt.

What you need

Butter or margarine for **greasing**

11 oz (325 g) fresh dates

5 oz (150 g) blanched almonds

4 oz (100 g) soft brown sugar

1 orange

4 eggs

¼ cup (25 g) superfine granulated sugar

½ tsp **ground** cardamom

1½ oz (40 g) butter

3 tbsp cornstarch

1 tsp confectioners' sugar to **dust**

What you do

1 **Preheat** the oven to 400°F (200°C).

2 Spread a little butter or margarine over a 9-in. (23-cm) loose-bottomed cake pan to grease it, and line it with waxed paper.

3 Cut the dates in half and take out the pits.

4 Put the almonds and brown sugar into a blender, and **blend** them until coarsely **chopped.**

5 Add the dates and blend until finely chopped, but not ground.

6 Using the fine side of a grater, **grate** the rind from the orange.

7 Cut the orange in half. Use a lemon squeezer to squeeze the juice from half of the orange.

8 Carefully crack open an egg. Keeping the yolk in one half of the shell, let the white drip into a bowl. Pass the yolk from one half of the shell to the other, until all the white has dripped out. Do this for all four eggs. If there is any yolk in the egg white, use a spoon to lift it out and discard.

9 **Whisk** the egg whites until they make soft peaks.

10 In a large bowl, **beat** the yolks with the granulated sugar and cardamom. Stir in the date mixture, butter, orange rind, 1 tbsp of orange juice, and cornstarch.

11 Using a large metal spoon, carefully **fold** in the egg whites.

12 Spoon the mixture into the greased pan and **bake** for 35–45 minutes, until the cake springs back when pressed.

13 Cool the cake in the tin for 15 minutes, and then place on a wire rack. Serve pieces dusted with confectioners' sugar.

Melon Fruit Salad with Rose Water and Mint

Farmers around the Nile River can grow many crops, including pomegranates and melons, because the land is crisscrossed with channels carrying water from the river. Rose water and fresh mint make this fruit salad especially refreshing.

What you need

2 small cantaloupes or any small melons
1 pomegranate
2 kiwi fruits
4 oz (100 g) seedless grapes
1 tbsp rose water or a few drops almond essence or orange flower water
1 tbsp lemon juice
1 tbsp honey
6 sprigs of fresh mint

What you do

1 Cut the melons in half. Scoop out the seeds with a spoon and throw them away.

2 Take a melon-baller (or a teaspoon, if you do not have one) and push it into the melon flesh. Twist the handle to make it cut through the flesh and make a ball. Do this to make balls out of the flesh of both melons.

3 Scoop out any melon flesh still left and **chop** it into small pieces. Keep the melon skins.

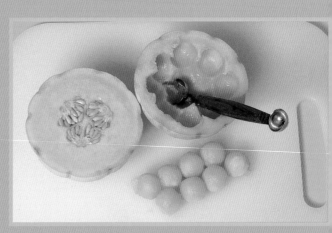

4 Cut the pomegranate in half, turn it upside down over a large bowl, and tap it with a spoon so that the seeds drop into the bowl.

5 Cut the skin off the kiwi fruits, and cut them into **slices**.

6 Put all the fruit into the bowl with the pomegranate seeds. Add the grapes.

7 In a small bowl, mix the rose water, lemon juice, and honey.

8 Rub two sprigs of mint between your fingers, and add them to the rose water mixture. Pour the liquid over the fruit.

9 **Cover** the bowl with plastic wrap and **chill** for 1 hour.

10 Using a teaspoon, take out the mint leaves and throw away.

11 Spoon the fruit into the melon skins, and **garnish** each one with a sprig of mint.

Baked Almond-Stuffed Apricots

Apricots are plentiful in Egypt. People eat them fresh, or dry them to use later. Egyptian cooks use apricots to flavor many dishes as well. If you cannot buy fresh apricots, use four fresh peaches or nectarines instead.

What you need

3 oz (75 g) granulated sugar
2 tbsp lemon juice
1 cup (225 ml) water
2 oz (50 g) **ground** almonds
1 oz (25 g) pistachio nuts, shelled
16 fresh apricots
Plain yogurt

What you do

1 **Preheat** the oven to 375°F (190°C).

2 Put the granulated sugar, lemon juice, and 1 cup (225 ml) water into a pan. Heat them gently until the sugar has **dissolved**.

3 Put the ground almonds into a bowl.

4 Roughly chop the pistachio nuts and stir them into the ground almonds. Stir in 2 tbsp of the warm, sugary liquid.

5 Cut a slit along the side of each apricot where the skin has a little groove. Gently pull out the pits.

6 Spoon a little nut mixture into the middle of each apricot. Lay the apricots in an ovenproof dish, with the slits facing upwards.

⚠ **7** Pour the rest of the sugary liquid over the apricots. **Cover** the dish with foil, and **bake** for 20 minutes.

8 Serve the apricots with a spoonful of the liquid and some plain yogurt.

YOGURT AND CHEESE

Plain yogurt is served with sweet foods in Egypt. Some people make soft cheese from yogurt. They pour it into a woven basket over a bowl and wait for the clear liquid, called whey, to drip through. The thick, milky curds left in the basket are a type of soft cheese.

Further Information

Here are some places to find out more about Egypt and its cooking.

Cookbooks

Braman, Arlette N. *Kids Around the World Cook!* New York: John Wiley & Sons, 2000.

Cook, Deanna F. *The Kids' Multicultural Cookbook*. Charlotte, Vt.: Williamson Publishing, 1995.

Pratt, Dianne. *Hey Kids, You're Cookin' Now*. Chattanooga, Tenn.: Harvest Hill Press, 1998.

Vezza, Diane Simone. *Passport on a Plate*. New York: Simon & Schuster, 1997.

Books About Egypt

Hart, George. *Eyewitness: Egypt*. New York: DK Publishing, 2000.

Osborne, Will and Mary Pope. *Mummies & Pyramids*. New York: Random House, 2001.

Wassynger, Ruth Akamine. *Ancient Egypt*. New York: Scholastic Trade, 1999.

Measurements and Conversions

3 teaspoons=1 tablespoon	1 tablespoon=½ fluid ounce	1 teaspoon=5 milliliters
4 tablespoons=¼ cup	1 cup=8 fluid ounces	1 tablespoon=15 milliliters
5 tablespoons=⅓ cup	1 cup=½ pint	1 cup=240 milliliters
8 tablespoons=½ cup	2 cups=1 pint	1 quart=1 liter
10 tablespoons=⅔ cup	4 cups=1 quart	1 ounce=28 grams
12 tablespoons=¾ cup	2 pints=1 quart	1 pound=454 grams
16 tablespoons=1 cup	4 quarts=1 gallon	

Healthy Eating

This diagram shows you which foods you should eat to stay healthy. Most of your food should come from the bottom of the pyramid. Eat some of the foods from the middle every day. Only eat a little of the foods from the top.

Healthy eating, Egyptian-style

Egyptian dishes often include fresh fruits and vegetables, because they grow so plentifully along the Nile River. Most meals include bread, but rice and vermicelli pasta are also popular. Egyptian cooks use eggs, nuts, and beans from the middle of the diagram a great deal. They are all good sources of **vitamins**. Traditional cakes can be very sweet, so they are only to be eaten in small portions occasionally.

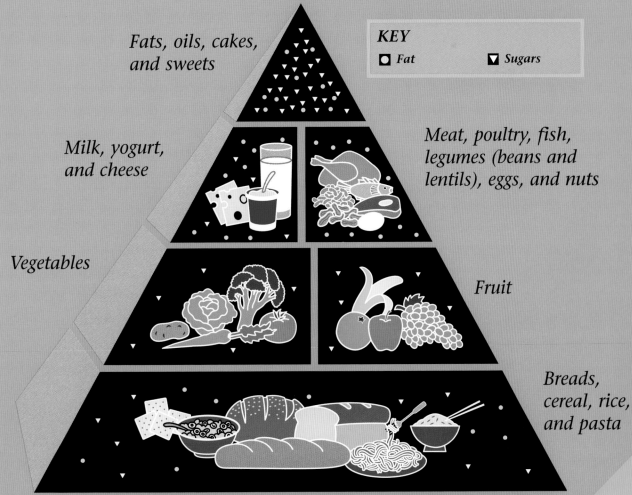

Fats, oils, cakes, and sweets

KEY
◻ Fat   ▾ Sugars

Milk, yogurt, and cheese

Meat, poultry, fish, legumes (beans and lentils), eggs, and nuts

Vegetables

Fruit

Breads, cereal, rice, and pasta

Glossary

archaeologist person who studies the past by looking at objects left behind by earlier peoples

bake cook something in the oven

beat mix ingredients together, using a fork or whisk

blend mix ingredients together in a blender or food processor

boil cook a liquid on the stove. Boiling liquid bubbles and steams.

broil cook under the broiler in the oven

chill put a dish in the refrigerator for a while before serving

chop cut into pieces using a sharp knife

coat cover with a sauce or batter

cover put a lid on a pan, or put foil or plastic wrap over a dish

dissolve mix something into a liquid until it disappears

drain remove liquid, usually by pouring something into a colander or sieve

dressing sauce for a salad

dry-fry cook at a high heat without any oil

dust sprinkle with confectioners' sugar or flour

fertile land that crops grow well in

flake break fish into flakes with a fork

fold mixing wet and dry ingredients by making cutting movements with a metal spoon

fry cook something in oil in a pan

garnish decorate food, for example, with fresh herbs

grate break something, such as cheese, into small pieces using a grater

greasing spreading a little margarine or butter on a baking tray or pan to stop the food from sticking when cooked

grill cook on an outdoor grill

ground make into a fine powder

knead press and fold with the hands

peel remove the skin of a fruit or vegetable

preheat turn on the oven in advance, so that it is hot when you are ready to use it

protein substance found in some food that living things need to grow new cells and replace old ones

sift remove lumps from dry ingredients, such as flour, with a sieve

simmer cook liquid on the stove. Simmering liquid bubbles and steams gently.

skewer long wooden or metal sticks for holding food

slice cut ingredients into thin, flat pieces

stir-fry cook foods in a little oil over high heat, stirring all of the time

toast heat under a broiler or in a toaster

toss mix ingredients, for example, in a salad

vitamins our bodies get these from food to keep healthy

whisk mix ingredients using a wire whisk

Index